Upside Down World

Also by Robin Sinclair and published by Ginninderra Press
The Clouds Go Down to Heaven
Haiku Diary
Now and Then

Robin Sinclair
Upside Down World

Upside Down World
ISBN 978 1 76109 133 9
Copyright © text Robin Sinclair 2021
Cover painting by the author

First published 2021 by
GINNINDERRA PRESS
PO Box 3461 Port Adelaide 5015
www.ginninderrapress.com.au

Contents

Once Upon a Time	7
About Painting	8
A Painting Happens	9
Painting now: the upside down world	10
Reflections	12
Art	13
The Colonial Painter: the statue and the man	15
Major Exhibition	16
Three Friends and a Painting Trip	17
Discovering Haiku	19
Wind	21
Haiku	22
About Writing	30
Correspondence	31
Spaces	32
The International Day of Not a Lot	33
Happiness Day	34
The International Day Without News	35
Take a Photo Day	36
The International Day of Poetry	39
Playing With Words	40
New Words	41
Election: Some Collective Nouns	43
The Year of the Rooster	44
The Garden	45
Apple Tree	46
Spring Walk in the Garden	47
Wattlebird and Foxglove	48
Raven	49
Ladybirds	50

Horoscope	51
Retreat	52
What I Saw At New Norcia	53
Night Drive in the Bush	56
After the Fire	57
Animals	58
Thoughts After a Visit to a Free-range Zoo	59
The Giraffe	60
Hippo	61
Lion	62
Galapagos Tortoise	63
Gibbon	64
Saying Thanks	65
In Memory of Terry Pratchett, died 2015	66
Two poems in memory of Mary Oliver, died 2019	67
This one for Mary Oliver is by my friend Kerry O'Regan	68
Memory	69
Abstraction	71
Three Years Later	72
Upside Down World: April 2020…	73
End of the World	74
Getting Ready To Go	75
I Think	76
Death	77
Twice Upon a Time	78

Once Upon a Time

Once upon a time
I climbed a waterfall
skidded my bike
and got a gravel rash
had scarlatina
watched my grandpa's gnarly fingers
cut up coupons
had to come out of *Lassie*
and sit sobbing on the stairs
because it was so sad
wrote a play and half a novel with a school friend
babysat the children of a poet
taught in a country town
where half the people shared a name
wasted a lot of time in chatter
but it wasn't wasted
and wrote a lot of letters
once upon a time.

Once upon a time
when I saw a splendid gum tree rearing to the sky
I'd run to paint it
capture it on canvas
make my mark
for others to enjoy.
Now it's enough to stand and wonder
take it in
make it a part of me.

About Painting

I do stand and wonder, but it seems that just taking it in is not quite enough. I still paint portraits of trees, trying to capture the spirit of the tree, the time and the place, an interpretation more than a photographic portrayal. The painting no doubt says as much about the way I like to see the world as it does about the trees themselves.

The act of painting can be a meditative exercise, taking away consciousness of the rest of the world and focusing attention on the now of the moment and the endeavour, drawing not only on technical knowledge and practice but upon the whole of the painter's life and experience and world view.

This is what I wrote about it twenty years ago.

A Painting Happens

A head full of ideas.
One is drawn out, and drawn out onto paper, tentative spider lines.
Push and pull the composition...that looks right.
Take a new canvas. Sweeps of charcoal rubbed and spread with fingers,
Darks expanded and erased.
Pungent whiffs of fixative to hold the web of liners in place, then pause...
A nervous hesitation. Take the brush.
A wash of ochre, blue and violet shadows, red earth red.
Excitement grows. Another brush, a handful.
Strokes of wet paint into wet and, fugitive, the shapes appear in painty wash,
Lights and darks, highs and lows and glows.
A half-seen glimpse of accidental brilliance...
A painting has begun.

Painting now: the upside down world

I'm doing a painting of the reflection of a clump of gum trees in a river. I knew from the start that it would be a challenge to make it more than pretty, which it could be because of the appealing subject, and to give some shape to the mass of branches mirrored in the moving water.

I began by sketching out the composition on to the canvas: the clump of trees taking up the top two thirds and the reflection in the bottom third. It looked wrong so I turned it upside-down so that now the reflections take up most of the space.

The top section – the trees, five trunks and their haphazard sprawl of branches against the blue background and scattered cloud of an Australian spring sky – is beginning to look convincing. Of course the branches only appear to be haphazard. According to the way they grow they are wonderfully disposed to fill the available space and to conform to what's around them. If it had been down to me as a gardener they would perhaps have looked tidier, a little more artistically arranged. In the picture I have tweaked them a bit, leaving out the ones that didn't suit my taste and adjusting the curve of a trunk to agree with my idea of a good composition.

Now to the bottom two thirds which still remain to be resolved. It's part of the way done, a half-rosette of shadowy foliage, a hint of supporting trunks and limbs. When I was there several months ago I looked at it with appreciation and some wonder and took a photo to aid my memory. The water seemed completely still. It was late afternoon shading into early evening and the moon was rising behind the trees.

When I began to paint, I wanted to capture the mirror-like quality of the reflection. But as so often happens the hand and the eye and the brush are moving me to a different interpretation. The brushstrokes are indicating a rippling and a shifting of light patterns, and I find that what is emerging is a movement that will take the eye of the viewer in a sweeping curve, and that the water-rippled flickering of the foliage in the reflection leads back and up to the crown of the trees on the banks, more solid and more real against the blue shadows of skeleton branches and leaves and the reassuring blue of the sky.

And back again.

Things look different in the upside down world.

Reflections

Late afternoon is draining out the colours
from the late spring sky.
All the sun that's left is lighting up the ivory and burnt sienna
of the trees along the river bank,
running its warming fingers up the trunks.
Twigs and branches seem to arch to catch the light,
cobalt shadows flicker in and out among the leaves.

But in the mirror of the water it's already dusk.
No sunlight here and just the ghosts of trees…

Art

The making of it and the loving of it
keep us whole.

Lovely and lyrical
true poetry can thrill the senses,
take out breath and lift our hearts,
or challenge and disturb.

Music finds the voices of the wind,
the scintillation of the stars
and makes us weep or dance.

Painting illuminates and satisfies,
asks the questions that perturb
and brings with it a sight of Yes!

Art,
as necessary to our lives
as bread and breath.

On a visit to Tasmania, we called at the small upper-Midlands town of Evandale, close to the farm where the famous colonial painter, John Glover, settled in the 1840s. Back in England, he had a distinguished reputation as a painter of landscapes, but when he was already in his sixties he made the decision to come to the other side of the world and join members of his family in the young colony of Van Diemen's Land. The home and studio he built are still there and have recently been restored. In Evandale there is a fine statue of him at work.

The Colonial Painter: the statue and the man

Mr John Glover, stocky elderly RA
stands four-square before his easel,
squints at the horizon,
holds his thumb up checking out the scale,
adjusts his palette and his expectations,
realigns his brain
from misty English skies and jewel-box greens
to something different,
the greens more muted and the sky more vivid and intense,
the trees that shed their bark in strips
and casually discard their leaves at will.

He likes it.

Major Exhibition

Big art for big messages…

In the gallery
a series of rooms
painted with midnight,
spaces leading into darkness,
a maze in which we lose ourselves
and find awareness.

Art…
the more it needs to be explained
the less it says.

Three Friends and a Painting Trip

The bush is radiating stillness.

In the dry creek lie
tumbled heaps of red round-shouldered rocks
the colour of the land
and drifts of gum leaves
ankle deep
a hundred shades from pale to rusty brown,
every one a work of art
sculpted by wind and insects,
origamied by the sun…
and just a memory of water.
All the greens have disappeared
siphoned off into the reservoir of spring.
Spiky clumps of desiccated grasses
wait for resurrection.

Sitting quiet, I paint,
the brush a focus for the eye, the hand,
the instinct.
Two flies and a goanna come to look.
Nearby some Peaceful Doves are calling 'Hollyhock'.

Meanwhile, two creek bends and a river gum away
a painter friend
by way of pencil, paper and imagination
delicately transcribes
some whorls and arabesques of shedding bark,
while in another place the third one
fills the pages of her book with watercolour,
luminous and limpid,
so that the soul glows out among the ancient trees.

Discovering Haiku

April 2019

About twenty years ago, I was introduced to haiku, the tiny Japanese verse form that is so small that it can be easily overlooked, dismissed as trifling, or even missed altogether. It is a kind of poetic hiccup that manages to encapsulate an Aha! moment in seventeen syllables or less. I loved it.

I am not the only one to have been captivated. Since it was introduced into English a century or more ago, it has swept the world. It has been imitated, copied, parodied and adapted; defended against change by outraged purists and taken over by others to provoke chuckles about anything from cats to spam. It can take the breath with its encapsulation of the moment, a perfect miniature. There is often a wry twinkle.

I decided to learn to make haiku by practising every day as I walked. We live in a beautiful part of the Adelaide Hills and walks near our small village can take me through the bush, by the creek and past farms and gardens. Every day, I tried to write at least one. The first were laboured and quickly discarded. Haiku need a lightness of touch. I tried to follow the pattern of syllables as set down by the early translators and practitioners — five in the first line, seven in the second and five again in the last. I counted them on my fingers as I walked, keeping in mind the useful model

> Writing a poem
> In seventeen syllables
> Is not very ea

After a while, I started to get the hang of it. I carried a small notebook and pencil with me, often stopping at the side of the road or beside a puddle or sometimes in the middle of a puddle to jot down the lines.

> After rain…
> ankle-deep in a pool that
> holds half of the sky

Or

> Walking on shadows
> my feet move in and out of
> flickering branches

When I got home, I sorted out the best arrangement of words, often changing the order but keeping the idea, and then transcribed them to a bigger book. Soon I had hundreds.

The very best thing about making haiku is that it has helped me to become a keen observer. Now, when I look at one I wrote years ago, it can take me instantly and vividly to that time and place.

On a trip to New Zealand, I kept a journal in haiku form, sometimes taking liberties with the form in order to tell a continuing story. This is likely to make some purists frown but I am entirely unrepentant. The Japanese poets who invented haiku centuries ago were whimsical and innovative. All poetic forms can be played with and I think haiku is ours to do with as we like; a gift to joy and imagination.

Walking is a good time not just for composing haiku but also for thinking. It helps to clear the mind and sort out directions. But the resolution comes with brush or pen in hand.

Wind

The wind as I walk
is wuthering the treetops
feathering my hair
finding its way into my head
and blowing out the cobwebs
rearranging thoughts
and huffing them away
to skitter like dead leaves into the gutter.

Haiku

Spring

new growth on old trees…
how the world renews itself
age to age to age

floating pink petals
dock themselves along the bank…
the creek chuckles by

brown wren on a twig
a small round fluffy bundle
of contentment

pulling out weeds…
what did they do to deserve this?
nothing but flourish

taken by surprise
or so it seems, a sleeping tree
bursts into flower

wisteria flowers…
a feast for the eye and a
snack for the rosella

spring gale…the fruit net
wants to take off for
Kangaroo Island

Still quite drab as yet…
he hasn't got his plumage on
the young rosella

Winter

somebody did it again!
…rearranged
the supermarket

with barely a sigh
the old apple tree branch
sinks into the hedge

bus chatter…
the air fills with intimate static…
I switch off

white cockatoos
huddling on telegraph poles
gathering mist

grey day, mossy post
lit by a robin moment…
a flicker of flame

everything stops
as we watch the hailstones bounce
off the windowsill

the mist comes down
enfolding us in silence
shutting out the world

early winter walk…
a festival of fungi
in pop-up displays

Autumn

after the downpour
bedraggled and bewildered
a baby ringtail

flashes of red…
firetail finches bob and scuttle
on the hunt for seed

a sudden autumn…
red gold leaves come and go
in a papery flurry

red leaves skittering…
a gust of autumn passes
across the gravel

the fire siren moans…
autumn is not so mellow
as we supposed

some yellow toadstools
turning themselves inside out
by the muddy track

rosella glowing
among the dark leaves breakfasts
on correa flowers

they may look holy
in their sombre plumage but
crows are atheists

Summer

the day warms up
and the skinks accelerate
skulk to scuttle

I waited all day
but the creative muse seems
to have missed the bus

we watch on TV
Sir David, the patron saint
of wonderment

not Peter Rabbit
but a black and white relative
pruning back the kale

'Into a pie!'
I say to the kids…not quite
but very tempting

reaching up as high
as I can stretch…green beans
racing for the sky

flies and goannas
might enter…please remember
to shut the door…thanks

two willy wagtails…
a black and white expression
of chirpy confidence

About Writing

After years of making and taking notes in biro and pencil, it came to me that it was time to buy a fountain pen.

Biros are for shopping lists and for making notes on the calendar.

Propelling pencils, especially the fine ones, are good for drawing: always sharp; the delicate line, the precision, the rubber on the end which can erase instantly; good for writing haiku which often need to be tweaked, words moving around interchangeably until at last they click into the best place. Good for writing and later erasing a name inside the cover of a book which, maybe, will turn out to be one that you didn't want after all.

But reflective writing requires a fountain pen. My first one marked the beginning of high school, a step up from the steel nibs and inkwells of primary school and the inky calloused fingers that went with them. They came with me to uni, and then into teaching, and then somehow the succession of fountain pens began to dwindle and finally to disappear, submerged by a rising tide of biros that seemed to move mysteriously from room to room, packing themselves into jars and handle-less mugs, hiding under piles of paper or in the fruit bowl, and disappearing under the fridge or through cracks in the floor, their numbers growing and decreasing with no apparent link to reality.

The pen I chose this time was spring green, beautifully and ergonomically fitted to the hand. Were fountain pens like this when I was fifteen? They are still the best for thoughtful correspondence.

Correspondence

Jane Austen in her letters to her sister
wrote pithily and wittily,
acerbically, perceptively
and often.
After her death Cassandra burnt them all.
Was it at Jane's request?
Who knows?
In any case
posterity is miffed.

Lavinia Dickinson
on the other hand
defied her sister Emily
and chose not to destroy her poems.
Whatever Emily
in Heaven and in retrospect
might think about it now
posterity is pleased.

So, would we want our thoughts and insights,
idle speculations, throw-away remarks
and casual gossip
read by just anybody?
No?
Well, as of now these words of ours
are out there in the Cloud for all to see.
And that's forever.

So Jane, and so Cassandra,
up there in a Cloudland of your own,
perhaps you got it right.

Spaces

In poems as in life
the gaps are as important
as the words.

Spacing:
time to breathe,
to taste the words,
to let the subtleties that passed you by
catch up and take you by surprise
making you draw a breath
or chuckle
or sit back.

Don't rush a poem.
Read it aloud.
Take time and let it infiltrate,
to fill your mind with wonder and your heart with warmth
or chill.
Rage and frustration have their place as well.

If boredom strikes
discard the poem
and then reread yourself.

The International Day of Not a Lot

It seems there is a designated Day for almost anything you can think of. Some are important and serious. Some are not.

Happiness Day

Today's officially 'Be Happy Day'.
Yesterday was set aside by some
for melancholy,
though we weren't told.

There is no day that celebrates embarrassment,
misunderstanding, rage,
frustration or despair.

But Happy is snappy,
let's all go with happy
and that will make the world
a better pace for generations.
Won't it?

But what to do with all the rest?
Well, feelings pass.
But that won't happen to Happy.
Will it?

The International Day Without News

It was a day without news.
Wars simply stopped.
Nobody was murdered, bashed or raped.
No traffic accidents occurred,
or fires, or floods.
As the news receded,
flowing out and disappearing like the tide,
the space was filled with gentle sunlight,
kind and unassuming people,
hopes and aspirations for a better life,
hand-knit jumpers,
bird song,
gardens and gardeners,
paddling in the sea.

No sport occurred
except for hopscotch, backyard cricket,
marbles, doodling and a little Scrabble.

TVs and radios went quiet.
MPs and commentators drifted to the beach.

The world was heard to sigh and then relax.

Take a Photo Day

Lots of people must have known about it
because there they were,
taking photos of themselves,
each other and their pets,
their coffee, what a work of art,
their meal, the table and the passersby,
the sky, the sunset and the funny cloud.

Perhaps they need to tell themselves
that they were there
and that they saw it,
so it must be real.
And so must they.

My mother loved photos. She had boxes of them. She put them into albums and took them out again and put them into other albums. In the early days, she wrote on the back of them in pen and later in biro, and sometimes she wrote on the front of them. At first she used photo corners. Some she stuck in with paste, and later on took them out so that they became thinned and papery where the glue had been. The corners became creased and tatty.

In the 1940s, she discovered that it was possible to paint colour on to black and white photos, so the chubby cheeks of toddlers became suddenly and luridly pink.

Her collection told the story of her life. There she was, with her five sisters in the school photos from the 1920s, the belts of their school tunics modishly dropped to hip line. There, in a shoebox, was a record of their exuberant, loving, squabbling teenage years, fresh-faced, robust and healthy, always laughing.

Next came the portraits taken during World War II, not laughing now but each sister in her new uniform smiling out at my grandparents: army, air force or nursing sister. Photographers must have done well in those days.

When at eighty-seven my mother had a stroke and had to move to a nursing home, I thought I could make her feel more at home by making a photo-montage of her children and grandchildren. I took time and care to choose them and place them in a large new frame. She was pleased with the idea and thanked me, but I could tell right away that I'd chosen the wrong photos. Within weeks, some had been removed and replaced and others added. A couple had been improved by outlining in ink. Within a year, the frame had disappeared and a large display board had taken its place. The number of photos, old and new, tatty, loved and creased had grown tenfold. They had been drawing-pinned, blutacked, cut down to size, and overlapped. Nothing archival going on here; she liked the hands-on approach. It was her life, her choice, her past and present all in one.

Photos are important.

The International Day of Poetry

Just for this day
    give up on media
    abandon screens
    and read a poem

    read another poem
    let it sink into you

    write a poem
    tear it up
    write a line
    write two lines

    is it a poem yet?
    how long does it have to be to be a poem?
    does it matter?

    feel a glimmer which
    with any luck
    might one day be a poem

Do the same tomorrow.

Playing With Words

Playing with words and rhymes is a lot of fun. Every year, new words come into use and are added to dictionaries. Others must get pushed out to make room for them. I wonder where they go?

New Words

They roll so neatly off the tongue
these brave new words.
So have they sprung
from inspiration and acuity,
an innate joy in ingenuity,
a neologismitic surge
born of the compelling urge
to fill a gap that's just occurred?

A word, a word, I need a word!

It's too easy to make fun of politics and politicians. The first of the following poems was written in the year of the last Australian federal election, and the second after the US presidential election of 2016. Was I too optimistic? I hope not.

Election: Some Collective Nouns

A squawk of pollies,
An indifference of voters,
A pursuit of journalists,
A chatter of commentators,
An excitement of psephologists,
A shock of jocks,
A vegie bed of Greens,
A disharmony of unions,
An oversupply of economists,
An alignment of editors,
A polarisation of opinions,
A plethora of promises,
A sinking of spirits,
A diminishment of hopes.

The Year of the Rooster

The game is up, the die is cast,
The day of doom is here at last,
The horse has bolted, bucked and jumped
And thrown its rider. We've been Trumped!
The vote was rigged, election fixed;
Feelings and metaphors are mixed.
Hopes and plans have turned to dust.
Throw up your hands! The system's bust.

We hear its whining everywhere,
The Vacuum Cleaner of Despair,
But don't lose hope and do not fear –
The Broom of Decency is here,
The Mop of Hope and Good Intent,
The Hearth Brush of Enlightenment;
And in your hand, to make a start,
The Feather Duster of Good Heart.

The Garden

Not far from our house are patches, sometimes hectares, of original bush: a scrubby underbrush, tall stringybarks, casuarina and callitris, a scatter of acacias and the occasional majestic stand of candlebarks; and in their season a froth of delicate flowering plants and native orchids. Our garden must have been like that 140 years ago, half an acre on a ridge arcing up from the creek and the village with a gentle slope falling away to the front and a steeper one at the back of the house. The block was cleared to build the house and make a 'proper' garden. Since then, it has been through several makeovers until now it has settled into being what most Australian gardens are today, a multicultural garden, a kind of United Nations of the plant world, with trees and shrubs, perennials and bulbs from every continent and many climates.

Towering over the house is an old apple tree.

Apple Tree

The tree
which never saw an orchard or a pruning saw
is reaching to the sky,
tossing in autumn squalls.
On a branch two spinebills flicker through the yellow leaves,
one upside down.
One blue wren
is lighting up a moody day.
Three rosellas ride the highest twigs
bracing against the breeze
until they're shivered off.

In last week's storm a branch was torn off at its base
and fell, giving us wood
to give a friend
who'll turn it into bowls.
The celebration of a hundred years of life
becomes a work of art.

Spring Walk in the Garden

The temperamental late-September winds
have combed the garden's hair,
raking out a tangled spill of brittle lichen-covered twigs,
shaking down camellia flowers
to make a satin-smooth pink petal snow
which makes our grandson leap with joy.
At the back door the morning sun
stirs a boronia to life.
It smells of spring.
The birds agree,
their celebration fills the air.
High in the pussy willow
lorikeets arrive to get their sugar hit
and carry on their squabbling while they sip.
The sleekly silver catkins of last week
have sparked with gold,
a fireworks display.

In the vegie bed the broad beans flower,
reliable and always on the job.
The rainbow chard looks fresh and keen,
the garlic, not so sure.
Plenty of parsley volunteers this year.
Asparagus gets set to go
and rhubarb races fatly forth.
Sweet peas on the trellis overtook the other kind
some time ago. This year
the feast is for the eyes.
Meanwhile on the bare-branched fig
tiny green balloons are popping out.
At ankle height a sweep of bluebells
spreads beneath the trees.

Wattlebird and Foxglove

Beside the door
a rusty wheelbarrow
full of earth
is fountaining foxgloves,
spikes of trumpets, purple, pink and mottled white,
each just the size for one fox paw to fit.

Foxes come and go at night
raiding chooks and eggs and digging up dead pets.
I never saw one yet look at a foxglove
or try one on for size.

But wattlebirds, they like the fit,
good for large honey eater bills.
Clinging to a spire and half its size
they sway and dip and feast.

Raven

On the edge of the bird bath,
predatory, black and glossy,
sits this descendant of the dinosaurs.

His eye – he has the topaz eye,
knowing, alert, intent.
His beak is polished ebony,
evolved to strike,
his claws, precise and delicate, brushstrokes of black
designed to clutch.
With one he holds the rim, secure.
The other has a dried-up piece of bread.
He dips the crust…three seconds…four…
into the water.
Then he politely eats.

Ladybirds

Late autumn
and the ladybirds are drifting in
to over-winter in a cosy spot.
We find a cluster, berry-like,
under the mantelpiece,
another in a corner of the ceiling,
and singly in the fruit bowl,
ornamental but at home.

In the coffee plunger, that was a surprise.

Ladybirds, or sometimes ladybugs
or even ladybeetles…
Ladyberries, that's the one I like,
And yes, they're ladylike,
demure,
tucking their wings beneath their shiny skirts,
good mannered in the best Victorian way,
knowing their place.
Inside.
Hoping that nobody will find them out.

Horoscope

So Mercury's in transit
and that means I can't go out
and must be careful what I say.

At least it isn't retrograde.
We know that retrospection
leads to introspection,
giving rise to incredulity
and then to doubt.

That's where I am today.
So Mercury, take note.
I'm going out.

Retreat

In the spring of 2018 and again in 2019, I spent two weeks at a Quaker retreat in New Norcia, WA. The place should be haunted by ghosts from its past but I didn't sense them. It is a small monastic town founded in the mid-1800s by a visionary Spanish Benedictine monk called Dom Salvado. In the spirit of the time, it was a mission to rescue the Indigenous people of the area and bring them to God, civilisation and a settled life. Like most ventures of its kind, there were times of heroic endeavour and times of what we now see as sabotage of a culture and a way of life. For many, despair; for others, hope. Everything in human experience is more complicated than we can either imagine or understand.

But now New Norcia and its peaceful setting is a beautiful place to spend a quiet week. I set out to write a poem celebrating the birds and got sidetracked by the history.

What I Saw At New Norcia

I didn't find the spirit of Salvado
hovering by his marble tomb
so solid in the church,
although it said his bones were there.

I think I sensed it by his statue,
arm upraised, the light of mission in his eyes,
looking across the land he loved and those he cherished here.
Beneath it is the gritty reddish soil.
Nearby are some eucalypts,
trunks glowing in the setting sun
Ivory and orange-gold and silver,
so much more real than any angel host.
I notice that his back is to the graveyard
where rows of metal crosses march away
telling the dates and lives of brothers who,
from far away, gave up their homes
and came to save the souls and change the lives
of those whose land this was.

Counterbalanced on the other side
are neat white wooden crosses, most unmarked,
of those who lived here and were rounded up
and civilised despite themselves,
all to the glory of a God they didn't know.

Everyone made sacrifices here.
In the long run maybe there was good enough
to balance out despair and wrong.
That's how the human story runs.

That isn't what I meant to say.
I meant to write about the ministry of birds.

From a gum tree high above us
two kookaburras take an overview.
No laughter, no. But possibly
a small reflective smile.
Under the ledge below the tower
some swallows nest,
swooping in elegant and ergonomic arcs
to feed their young,
They like to be where people are,
not so much for our company
as for the shelter we provide;
a tiny graceful counterpoint to human clumpiness.
The ring-necked parrots in the grass
are totally at ease with us,
the trees, the breeze, the insects and themselves,
an unselfconscious testament to self belief.

A pair of herons guard the weir,
awkwardly graceful as they flap and gangle
from the water to the trees
and croak their harsh, surprising cry.
In the scrub a host of small, anonymous
and busy birds flit and forage in the leaves,
fluting their sweet and piercing calls
in voices bigger than themselves.
I don't know what they're called.
Ornithologists have named them
but that isn't what they call themselves.

Not far from where I sit and write and think
under a venerable tamarisk
a bird is perching on the fence.
Unremarkable and slight it treats my casual interest
with indifference. And then it hops and bobs and turns –
a crimson flash of startlement!
A red-capped robin. Flick! He's gone.

Each one of these is perfectly evolved to fill its niche.
People are different.
We fit in more awkwardly.
Down here on the ground we human beings slowly pace
and think and write and meditate to find our way,
and all these things flow into us:
the sunlit sky, the cooling night, the comforting unfolding dark,
the air that's heavy with the scent of eucalypt and honey;
and the warm concern of all of us for each of us,
reaching out arms to hold each other up.
We find the Spirit here.
And underneath it all
the orchestration of the birds.

Night Drive in the Bush

The car drifts almost silently
through the almost blackness,
a tunnel of dark beneath the overhanging trees.

It's late and we are quiet,
voices still but eyes alert and watchful
for the sentinels which haunt the verge,
dim shapes that loom or leap
making us brake and swerve and almost stop.

We're running scared.
They're not,
not knowing that a sudden leap can end in death.
This is their time and place
and we're intruders.

After the Fire

After the bushfire stillness came
falling like the sombre snow of ash.
Animals had fled or died.
No birds called except for one,
a crow, black as the trees,
wailing its mournful cry into the drifting smoke.

In a while the rains returned
sifting into the ashes,
settling and soaking,
seeking out the roots,
trickling down the charcoaled trunks,
rinsing clean the reddish-gold of newer, smoother wood.
And up and down the trunk,
from base to branch,
the new green life began to shoot.

Animals

Animals are wonderfully made, endlessly fascinating and beyond our comprehension. As humans, we can't help projecting our own qualities and ideas on to them. Quite wrong, of course.

Thoughts After a Visit to a Free-range Zoo

Rhinos have gravitas.
They stand four square
and stop the world from tilting.

Cheetahs on the other hand
take lightning leaps
and keep the planet spinning.

Meerkats guard our backs,
eyeball the skies
and stop the aliens from getting in.

The wise orang-utan
disguising its sagacity, intelligence and love of peace
delights us as a clown.

The zebra's purpose is to entertain
and to distract us from…
so what was that again?

It's not the guide who told us this.
I worked it out myself.

The Giraffe

Long legs asprawl
mean a long neck
to reach the water with a long long tongue.

And length means gangle,
as in legs,
and grace,
as in the curving neck,
and practicality,
as in the looping licorice of the tongue.

Last of all,
and this is a surprise,
the melting looks from under lowered lids,
and long mascara'd lashes.

Hippo

'If you prick us, do we not burst?'

Does somebody inflate them when they're born
so that they bob and surge in rivers,
even swim with stumpy legs?
Here is an animal that fits into its skin
with imperturbability.
No wrinkles here.

Lion

He lies around all day
and sleeps.
Does not go to the gym.
He lolls at leisure in his lair,
yet when he stalks and prey is near
he leaps to action like a deer.
I ask of those who envy him,
does this seem fair?

Galapagos Tortoise

Its rolling gait a silent rumble,
its face a quintessential grumble,
a prehistoric toothless mumble.
Here before we first began
it may need luck to outlast Man.

Gibbon

An offhand acrobat,
casual accomplishment as natural as breath.
This is as close to flying as an animal can get.
Uses a branch to launch its swing,
a fingertip to slow it
and instinctive grace to know exactly how and when to fall.

Swing, oh swing, my fellow creature.
How I envy you!

Saying Thanks

We all have writers we love and owe a lot to. We respond to some because they reflect our own way of looking at life, but there are others who have helped to transform the way we see the world. Here are my thanks to two of them, about as different from each other as they could be, but both loved by many.

In Memory of Terry Pratchett, died 2015

Out there in Space the Turtle glides.
On its back the Discworld rides;
and somewhere in the multiverse
where all the Pratchett fans converse
a multitude of folks diverse
share sad laments and mournful looks
at thoughts of no more Pratchett books.

The Disc is our alternate world
as much as his. On it we're swirled
through plots fantastic, mad inventions,
neat deflation of pretensions,
good and dastardly intentions,
and see with joy the interplay
of magic with the day to day.

We laugh with Pratchett at ourselves
disguised as witches, guards and elves.
We chuckle as with gleeful shrug
he pulls the metaphoric rug
from politician, priest and thug.
We'll miss you Terry as you trot
with kindly Death to – who knows what?

Two poems in memory of Mary Oliver, died 2019

She taught us to see nature through her eyes,
fresh and lovely and astonishing;
sometimes fierce; acknowledging that death
is part of life.

She helped us see the wonder of the smallest bird,
the hunting owl,
the foibles of a dog,
the nameless lurker in the pond
that sends a shiver down the spine.

She wrote on our behalf the pain of ageing
in a creaking frame,
and of acceptance,
and of life transmuted
through the wonder of a child.

This one for Mary Oliver is by my friend Kerry O'Regan

Who will tell us now
to slow our pace
steady our gaze
be wild. Wilful.

To turn sharp right and see at once
the new, the old, the unexpected
to bring us up short
abandoning humbug and pretence
leaving only trees, small creatures, wild geese,
and the soft unyielding nakedness of our own souls.

Memory

We're floating in a cloud of memories
and in it float the jigsaw puzzle pieces of our lives
that drift and rearrange themselves
into a pattern that we know and like.

The very air we breathe is memory.
But no, we are our memories
and to lose them or lose part of them
is like a fraying of the edges of ourselves.

One of my closest friends has Alzheimer's. Here are two poems, written three years apart after visits to her far away in another state.

Abstraction

Playing Scrabble with my friend of fifty years
I see with sadness that she's losing it.
'Is this a word?' she says.
She knows it's word-shaped,
so it might be.
But it's not.
Searching for words
she finds that many seem to be
deleted from her memory.

She asks with tender care, 'How is your health?'
and listens every time, attentively,
as though she's never heard it all before,
although she has, four times this afternoon.

Timidity replaces her exuberance.
She quails at going out, except to walk and walk;
at home retreats into the painting that she loves
and rediscovers endlessly, excitedly,
techniques that she uncovered in the past.

Some years ago she started painting abstracts,
shapes for the pleasure of themselves,
colours that flow and intersect,
accidents that bring delight.
In that chaotic, undefined, exhilarating world
she finds the self she's lost.

Three Years Later

I know that in there are the memories
but what the eyes are saying is, 'I'm lost…'
Words are disappearing
   noun by noun
and scrap by scrap the knowledge ebbs away.

It's said the eyes are windows to the soul.
Where is the joy, the creativity that marked her life?
Gone into her family,
the paintings, music, friendships and the endless meals,
atoms of herself dispersed.

What's left?
The loving self that still connects.

What's gone?
The actions and accomplishments are done,
enjoyed, acclaimed and left behind.
The sense of self…almost…not quite…

'I'm lost.'

Upside Down World: April 2020, during the long lockdown

Here cocooned within our nests
we wait the crisis out,
inhabiting with some surprise
the spaces in our lives…
a mix of consternation and delight.

Some fill the gaps with social media or books,
some with TV,
some with an avalanche of busyness.
Some glory in the solitude
and rediscover, reassess and reinvent their lives.

A world turned upside down,
taken to pieces,
shaken up,
then put together – how?

Meanwhile
in the other world
millions lose their livelihood,
and millions die.

End of the World

Our planet is a tiny speck,
part of a galaxy that drifts
among a million million galaxies.
Is it – are we – as special as we think?

It is, as we are, each unique,
complexities of love and hope and fear,
and when we die a small but poignant gap
exists for just a moment
and then closes with a sigh
and life goes on,
vibrant and complex as it always is
but just a little different.

And so it is with every creature that exists,
with every species that becomes extinct,
a tragedy. And yet the gap will close
and something just as wonderful
may take its place.

And if we do, by malice or ineptitude
destroy our world
the Universe will sigh…but
far beyond our vision or imagining
the wonder will go on.

Getting Ready To Go

The years have trickled, raced and dawdled past
and here I am, drifting towards the end of life.
Drifting, not trotting.
One day soon I might slip quietly away,
a dwindling stream skeining itself across the sand to reach the sea.
I might drop off a cliff without a chance to yell my startlement.
I mightn't even know.
If I return to where I started from
I think I won't.
Or it could be a slow uncomfortable journey,
rather like a tedious airline flight across the world,
something to be endured.
It's not what I'd prefer.
Just so you know.

I Think

I think he thought
his wife would say no,
on no account,
there's still a lot to live for
and I couldn't bear it…

That's why he didn't ask
or talk it over.
I think he felt he had to go;
that they would be more hurt
more desolate
if he tried to explain to them.

I think he thought
if they said no
he wouldn't have the strength to leave.
That's what I think.

But then, what would I know?

Death

At the end of life
there's one thing I can say with certainty:
I'm glad I came.

Everything ends.
The rocks of ages go to dust,
leaves fall and trees decay,
animals and people die.
Even the universe, which started with a bang
will in the course of time blink out.
Death is a part of life.
But atoms never vanish
so they say,
and at the end ours will rejoin
the stars they came from.
In a way we've always been here,
and will always be.

We also know that we don't go
as long as there are loved ones to remember us.

I like to think of death as moving on
from the kaleidoscope of life
into a deep and dreamless sleep.
And so it will be, in a way.

Or death, is it the door
as some do say
into the next adventure?
Wait and see.

But in the meantime here I am.
I'm glad I came.

Twice Upon a Time

Twice upon a time
I made a friend and married him
lived in interesting places
travelled round the world
and learned some other cultures
had a family and a lifetime's education
from my children
stacked a room full with my paintings
pulled and dug a million eager weeds
planted trees that now reach skyward
filled a journal with obituaries for more
read a lot of books
and read some more
wrote and spoke and heard a lot of words
and laughed a lot
learned to love the silence.

Twice upon a time
I learned that I had plenty yet to learn
and not much time to learn it.
What will happen thrice upon a time?

www.ingramcontent.com/pod-product-compliance
Lightning Source LLC
Chambersburg PA
CBHW062150100526
44589CB00014B/1764